SNAKE LANGUAGE

Nigel Wells

Published by
Llyfrau Cambria Books, Wales, United Kingdom.
Cambria Books and Cambria Stories are imprints of Cambria Publishing Ltd.
Discover our other books at: www.cambriabooks.co.uk

the squeal of nerves

(glass on tin)

the breath dragged back

(snake language)

By the same author:

The Winter Festivals, Bloodaxe Books 1980
Wilderness/Just Bounce, Bloodaxe Books 1989
Walesland/Gwaliadir, with parallel Welsh translation by Caryl
Lewis, Gomer 2006
Sly Deeds (Performance Texts), Cambria Books 2024

Cover Images from The Procession by Meri Wells
Back cover photo by Stephen Florence
Dancer's Piece from *The Glory Reel* first published in *Sly
Deeds*

CONTENTS

EQUILIBRE

These poems were commissioned by Jane Lloyd-Francis and Georges Dewez for performance by readers and riders at Carreg Dressage, Abercegir during 1994 and 1995.

HORSE IN FLAMES
A Balkan folk tale

This is the horse of fame
this is the horse of flame
and these are the eyes
of the horse of blame
these are her eyes.
Oh, they are furnace gates
and fear and fire roll down from them.
This is the horse in flame
her mane in flame
her sides in flame
who cries through flame.
This is the horse no name
and her hooves drum sparks and pain
as she runs upon ground and in air
and she drips fire everywhere.

This is the corn and these are the crops
that burn as the horse of flame goes by
and these are the people who tend
the crops, who argue and blame and watch them

die as the fire of the horse of flame goes by.
And these are the houses and this is the town
that blackens and falls, that tumbles down as
the people wail and fight and die as the eyes
of the horse of flame go by.
Oh, they are furnace gates
and fear and fire roll down from them.

And the horse no-name, poor horse, poor horse
burns with terror, burns with loss
and fire eats her will, fire eats her voice
as she runs and she runs and she runs
without choice
and yellow flame and red despair
spill from her sides everywhere.

But a child of the town
who is sad for the pain
of the horse of flame
gives her a name and calls
that name and sings and sings
and sings all the shame
from the horse of blame
the horse of flame and

blankets with song
the fire and the wrong
and the horse is calm.
For the child and the song
and the name are balm
that quench the fire
in the horse of flame.
But oh, her eyes were furnace gates
and fear and fire rolled down from them.

So the fire dies down in
the crops and the town and
the people stare at the ashes there
and root in the rubble of what remains.
And this is mine, no it's mine
and they squabble and fight once again.
Oh fire breeds fire and it stains.

And the child holds the reins
of the horse that was flame
and cries "see her eyes see her eyes".

Oh, they are cool and beautiful
and tears roll down from them.

LOOK BACK

Look back.
There is a pathway
dark and brilliant
its length
measured in millennia.

That
is the path of history
glorious and despicable
and paved
with the bones of the horse.

*

The first horse
was Eohippus

which grazed
strange grass
stripped bark
from queer trees.

The first horse

Eohippus

which stood
a bare three hands

and ran
on toes not hooves

riderless.

The first horse.

　　　　*

Look back
thirty thousand years before
certain events at Bethlehem
at cave walls under
Sierra de Yeguas

long necked beasts
depicted in red
hunted for meat

Look back
ten thousand years
before that carpenter

the same caves
strong backed creatures
in proportion and conformation
able to carry a male adult
depicted in black

Equus Stenonius
the functional warhorse.

*

Look back
lines of men
break, fall away, fall

a five foot axe
wielded from ground level
being no match
for a hatchet swung
by a rider
down

Look back.
Duke William's useful cobs
stitched into perpetual gallop
by the goodwives of Bayeaux

John of Gaunt's lumbering giants
mail plated, carrying
thirty stone of armoured knight

Charles Stuart's gift horses
taller still, but balanced, agile
precision bred for the firearm age

Look back
lines of horse
versed in gait and turn

charge, wheel, evade
disciplined, tactical
the Great Horse
schooled in movement

piaffe, levade, capriol.

THE HORSE MIRRORED

There was a place
so utterly bare
it could be
perfect peace
or pure terror.

And in it was a horse
and in it was a man
and no horse
or man had ever before met
in this place or another.

*

In another place.
The sparks fly
the anvil rings
the angels sigh
the devil sings.

Spark of life
spark of death
angel's strife
devil's breath.

The devil sows
the devil weeds
the devil grows
the devil breeds.

Hammers swing
flash dancing imps
a horse takes wing
the devil limps.

And hoof burns
and horn welds
the devil turns
the devil gelds.

Some creature moans
some beast awakes
these are the bones
the devil makes.

The sinew wound
the axe whet
out of the ground
the devil's pet.

       *

Upon a time
a man walks a horse
his new found friend
and he thinks -

I will plait rope
trim leather
shape cloth
shave brass

I will dress you
in finery and appliance
and this will be the measure
of my love
and my control

and your acceptance
and your pride
will be the measure
of your love
and your control

*

The devil mouths the angel's song
the angel's tears are black
the pretty horse on dainty feet
hears cloven hooves that clack.

Always the hardening of a heart
always the soul gone slack
as from a recess in the eye
another eye glares back.

This is how it is
in mineral oil night
the great herds graze
the singular mare also.

This is how it is
in each and every breast-bone beats
the bright blood and the dark
for each embroidered field, a knacker's yard
for every stone an ark.

The sweet mouthed filly flicks her tail
the stallion broods on love
as sleep falls into wakefulness
as under marks above.

The inward motion meets the outward move
they turn and turn about
what's more strange than double-blood
the whisper in the shout.

The beast will ride upon the horse
the horse spur on the beast
and one shall tell of appetite
and one shall set the feast.

The devil flaps his angel wings
the angels shake their tails
as hell cries fit to quench its fire
and all of heaven wails.
This is how it is.

*

The waxy brand of flame
imprints the horrid heart
engulfs the sweet
an odious distinction but
that is just what fire does.

Horse, rider, counterpart
met with fire
and fire was called nothing
for it was nothing
just fire.

And horse with man
accepts fire, just
is that unnatural
or is that trust?

16

Maybe, perhaps
horse knew fire before
man's first scufflings
with spark, with stone, with stick.

Maybe, millennia since
a hoof rang rock
and briefly lit this mess
perhaps the horse in happy dark
found fire virtueless.

Fire on fire
burning, burning.

For some it glowed, was everything
the hearth, the. life, the muse.

For some it hurt and terrified
and had no earthly use.

All in all
is just what fire is
fire is.

After fire comes water
the cascade down the rock
the trickle from the spout
the bead of sweat.

I sing the song of the water-horse
who sails the under-tide
who races the clouds
who snorts and the moon rolls by.

I sing the song of her longing
not knowing what that may be
but knowing
that tilt of hoof
and set of head
a fragrant mouth
echo the dew and the sea.

I sing the song of the water-horse
for the cool reverse of fire
for the joy of a pool's reflection
for heartbeat at bursting sky.

The water-horse song
is a deep tra la
which spangles the earth
with thin clear blood
with dousing rain
and all that these are worth.

*

The other side of things
our homely fear.

The reflection in the mirror
not quite right, or us.

That mirror is a lair
the image is a lure.

A horse reflection stirs
flexes for the test
prepares in its stable
braces in its nest.

This is where this lives
this is what this is

a horse deranged
devil trained
a horse changed

      *

One to make ready
two to make hay
three to make horses
black, white and grey.

I ride my little hobby horse, white and well shod
she'll carry me for always nidity nod
carry me for always and roundabout
if she falls down then I'll cry out
up again hobby horse rise like yeast
nidity nodity my black beast.

Riddle me, riddle me, riddle me rare
what is dark but also fair
riddle me, riddle me, what must share
heart of shadow, heart of glare
nidity nodity our grey mare.

Stick horse, ribbon horse
how do you play?

do you have to fight yourself
to live another day?
Answer?
Yes.

                    *

Do you hear them?
the squeal of nerves
(glass on tin)
the breath dragged back
(snake language)

the rustle of dry tongues
the slow knock of teeth

and all the while
that awful muscle in the chest
(some engine in an oily shed)
thudding, quickening.

Do you hear them?
instinct's grate
reason's scratchy call.

They are the noises you shall hear
(the clink of fear and more)
if you should war, should fall.

Oh hold this close and hold it dear
let horse and man dance free
let chaos bow to melody
sing out, sing hard, sing clear.

What we have here
is a water skeleton.

What we have here
is a thing fire ravaged.

What we have is a version of a horse
(something appallingly sad).

What we have is this:
and it is masked
and it is unmasked
and it is secrecy
and it is show

and it is hideously sad
and now you know.

So
there was a place
there was a horse
there was a man.

And there was some other thing
and that was from some other place
and that was arse about face.

And that lived for them
and that lived off them
lived

still lives
that dark derangement sleeps
fitfully in the light
uneasy in the night
since and forever
goodnight.

SCALES

INTRO
for Will Kaufman

we commence to drink whiskey
fiddle faddle
Martin Hayes for sweetness
Kevin Burke for energy
sez you
ah play me a little Shady Grove
slide me away
Ry Cooder in Dublin

slow is smooth
smooth is fast
get a metronome
tick goes our past

funeral songs
come all ye's
the Parting Glass
yeah yeah yer arse

27

oh de wimmins de wimmins

yas yas yas

junk food, movies, beer

yo, Willy Boy is here

been a while

hey

listen to this.........

TOOK A RAZOR TO IT

I came up for air and saw love hanging around
Stuff you find when you put your head above ground
Down here we don't do that, don't give it a glance
But in a funny mood on a funny day I took a chance
   Crazy thing to do and I knew it
   Later I took a razor to it

Should've stayed underground, stayed down below
Love never go there, don't ever show
I walked in the open with my head in the air
Love turned its light on, I got caught in the glare
   Knew for sure I was gonna rue it
   Later I took a razor to it

Love took my skin off, hung it over a chair
I stood in my bare bones, heart bloody and rare
Love said you'll like this, it hurts but its nice
Burns you like fire and freezes like ice
   Yeah? take it, I said, and go chew it
   Later I took a razor to it

I don't really do this I was trying to say
I'm not from around here just out on the stray
Love kept applying the cold and the heat
Red hair and green eyes and a smell that's so sweet
  Damn! I said, I think I just blew it
  Later I took a razor to it

A jewel of a face, a wreath of a smile
All knowing grace, deep hidden guile
Love standing up there directing the show
Saying, pick any straw son, it's your choice you know
  There was a short straw and I drew it
  Later I took a razor to it

I took a razor to it, thought I beat it
But love's a tough one you can't defeat it
I jumped back under, left love up there
Least I thought I did but love don't play fair
I got this pain now and it won't quit
Like my heart's swoll so it won't fit
  But I can fix that - just take one slit
  Believe I'll take a razor to it

SALTLESS

The sun in you, the rain in me
Terrapin slides through a saltless sea
Love is remuneration
The geese run ragged, the cats all flee
Terrapin slides through a saltless sea
Love's our expectation

Your skin, my eyes
This life that one
Big words small cries
That life, this one

A green owl flies in your throat for glee
Terrapin slides through a saltless sea
Love turns decoration
A tangle in the net, a scuffle in the tree
Terrapin slides through a saltless sea
Love becomes mutation

Your scent, my breath
That life, this one
Small heart, big death
This life, that one

The snake can't move for ecstasy
Terrapin slides through a saltless sea
Love's a fine damnation
The ants wind home, the dogs go pee
Terrapin slides through a saltless sea
Love's an end quotation

The cold in you, the chill in me
Terrapin slides through a saltless sea

ALL TALKED OUT

Lying in a rented bed
Space balls rolling in my head
I can't cry and I can't shout
Dumb as dumb and all talked out

You say words are how we're made
Words our only stock in trade
Well I know that and I don't doubt
But lover I'm done and all talked out

You've got your life, I've got mine
And we've got this life in between
We can't wear it, we can't flout it
Mostly we just talk about it

We think we've covered every angle
Wrung them all out through the mangle
But always one more way to say
Tomorrow, now, yesterday

Pump them up or mince them down
What if? what next? the words go round
Should we? dare we? round and about
Lover I'm done and all talked out

Lying in a rented bed
I hear you leave, your careful tread
Hear my voice as you reach the door
Same time next week, we'll talk some more

PLEASE

There are leaves on the pathway, work to be done
The next life is hidden by the moon and the sun
I don't need this, I want this, I can't, but I must
Turn a field full of plenty to an acre of dust

Well I know how the tree feels with a frost to the core
And I know how a child eats in the world of the poor
The water we're made of the sea in the bone
Warm us and wash us and help us to home

I touch the ring on your hand, your collar, your cheek
Please stop me, please let me, please speak, no don't speak
The face in your face makes the slightest incline
I fall on your mouth you fall into mine

Well, I know how the tree feels with a frost to the core
And I know how a child eats in the world of the poor
The water we're made of the sea in the bone
Warm us and wash us and help us to home

Well, you came on the back of a nightbird to me
And stepped down so lightly, so gracefully
We have what we have for better or worse
Something's not nothing and a prayer's not a curse

Though I follow your fragrance, a fool in a hearse
Something's not nothing and a prayer's not a curse
The water we're made of the sea in the bone
Warm us and wash us and help us to home

END TIME

The back end of winter the thin start of spring
I am waiting for heaven or the telephone to ring
Each is the other so either will do
But neither is paid for so they're not likely to

This is forever I heard someone say
This is as good as it gets
Some spook out there coming to call in your debts
When there's no way you ever can pay

The tail end of loving the snout end of hurt
I used to be clean now I scratch at this dirt
Crouched in the tub just holding the soap
The water turned off and six inches of rope

This is forever I heard someone say
This is as far as it goes
What can you give us to stave off the blows
When you've nothing we want anyway

The dull end of daytime, the dark start of night

I am leaking my colour, I am losing the light

My strength's repossessed and taken away

My last words deemed worthless and left for the dray

And here comes that bring-out-your-dead cart

I have to climb on I think

We are only as strong as our own weakest link

And for most that link is the heart

Oh this is forever I hear myself say

I have paid, I can't pay, I will pay

BAD NERVES

I see your foot flick like the tail of a cat
I see your hands fold and unfold in your lap
I see that look form in the back of your eyes
I feel my throat turning dry

Here comes another confrontation
Another in our endless permutation
I get ready for whatever variation
I start preparing the lie

I feel that prickle in the base of the brain
I feel my nerves jump when you mention a name
I wonder if any of this stuff is on show
And how much do you know

We square up for further aggravation
A few tight rounds of pain and degradation
Mostly they just end in more frustration
There is no killer blow

Only this time your voice grates like steel rubbed with sand
I feel myself falling, I forget how to stand
Later I get up and find you on the floor
You're no problem no more

I say some words for you my close relation
As I drop you in the skip behind the station
I'm going to meet my other situation
And my blood starts to roar

CAPRICCIO

THE BRIG ARONWY

Oh it's of the brig Aronwy boys her story I'll relate

She weighed and sailed from a Western port in the summer of ninety eight

Bound for the fleet and the flagship on station at Gibraltee

With the Admiral's favoured lady on passage by decree

They'd not sailed far when this lady gay and the captain lost their pride

They sank in love so deep in love they vowed they'd set aside

So damned in love they swore they'd leave all duty home and kin

Make sail to the edge of the world to live off robbery and the wind

Oh captain fine and lady fair together made such show

They turned the heads of the officers and the hearts of the tars below

They poured such silvery words then into those sailors ears

Saying take your leave of the king's navy and we'll go as buccaneers

43

Then madly did the crew declare to serve at the pirate trade

Honour forgot they threw in their lot with the captain and his jade

They pledged they'd fill Aronwy with gold and precious stones

And change the crossed white ensign for the black with skull and bones

Now men will stray for treasure boys and stray for a woman's charms

Forswear all obligation, be blind to grief and harm

But the heart of a ship is true my lads, a ship will bear no shame

For the soul of the sea and the rights of man are measured in her frames

English lady, King's own men their bloody oath had made

To forsake their own country and rove as renegade

And many the coins and ingots piled in Aronwy's hold

But the heart of the ship grew heavy while the hearts of her crew grew cold

Oh the Aronwy sailed a year or more upon the rolling deep

And many a loaded merchantman was sent to a long sea sleep

While the heart of the proud Aronwy grew heavy as iron bar

Till it chanced in the winter of ninety nine she bore past Baltiza

The captain and his lady love lay in each others arms

When the steersman at the gale watch gave out a wild alarm

The ship has turned her head around she will not answer helm

She bears for the reef off Baltiza and is like to overwhelm

Then captain, crew and lady gay all cursed in disbelief

For the ship lay on to the rocky isle, the raging surf and the reef

The wheel was aright, the sails set fair to reach far off the shore

Yet she drove for the rock, drove for her doom and would not answer more

Oh it's of the brig Aronwy that foundered and went down

That took with her the faithless crew each one of them to drown

Off Baltiza she broke her back, she broke her heart as well

And her captain and his bold lady rolled under down to hell

For men will stray for treasure boys and stray for a woman's charms

Forswear all obligation be blind to grief and harm

But the heart of a ship is true my lads a ship will bear no shame

For the soul of the sea and the rights of man are measured in her frames

DRINK YOUR WHISKEY

I was working the roads when,
'tween Carrick and Glen
I first set eyes upon her
She was carrying a can and I thought meself then
That the sun it barely outshone her
I leant upon me spade for to watch her parade
And I knew I just had to win her
So I said me fair miss if you give me one kiss
You'll find that I'm no beginner
She turned her dark head looked at me and said
Young man can you drink whiskey
For you may kiss like the devil be a giant with your shovel
But young man can you drink whiskey

For whiskey is the water, a father's favourite daughter
And whiskey is a mother's only son
Whiskey's our salvation, our hope, our occupation
Whiskey's all you need when said and done
So of liquor from the grain I'll ask you once again
Young man can you drink whiskey

Oh I'm the lad for that I said and raised me hat
A glass in the hand is me joy
Others surely drink it but I can fairly sink it
For whiskey girl I'm your only boy
So we finished off her can and went to see her mam
Her da being dead from his liver
We hoped she would agree to the daughter marrying me
Our hearts were all of aquiver
Mam had a little think then took a little drink
Said young man you may feel frisky
But I raised me daughter right she needs it every night
Young man can you keep her in whiskey

For whiskey is the water, a father's favourite daughter
And whiskey is a mother's only son
Whiskey's our salvation, our hope, our occupation
Whiskey's all you need when said and done
So of liquor from the grain I'll ask you once again
Young man will you keep her in whiskey?

We were married by the still so we could drink our fill
The whiskey it was flowing
Then I said me darling wife on me whiskey drinking life
To the bedroom we'll be going

So we lay side by side the husband and the bride

She said she loved me dearly

I said I love you too let us do what lovers do

And that's what we did - well nearly

Don't ask how it was done but we brought forth us a son

And he's the dead spit of me

A spanking little lad who loves his mam and dad

But more he loves his whiskey

For whiskey is the water, a father's favourite daughter

And whiskey is a mother's only son

Whiskey's our salvation, our hope, our occupation

Whiskey's all I need when said and done

So of liquor from the grain I'll tell you all again

Be sure and drink your whiskey

Oh that liquor from the grain I'll say it once again

Why thank you mine's a whiskey.

DANCER'S PIECE
from "The Glory Reel"

Cowboys come and hear a story of the power
and the glory. Of death and great adventure
shining crime. How it was for one gunslinger
side by side with his dead ringer. Beyond the law,
below that borderline

Oh anyone of four or five, near two parts dead
just half alive. Would recognise the tale I have to tell
Most any of the top-notch guns, the badland's
universal sons. Would know I say it true and say it well

It was in the town of Gutshot,
Sheriff Johnson tied the hang knot
And placed it round the neck of someone's pa
Then he slapped old Dollar's but end
and so lawfully he did send
That pappy where a light shone deep and far

And legal-like the neck snapped, and festive
like the crowd clapped
An artist chalked a likeness of the head
The soul strung for the bye and bye,
heard as it flew a tiny cry
Somewhere was birthed a boy child in its stead

That boy came to his damned senses, grew and
grew and learned his tenses
Learned how to walk the line but walk it skew
Learned the word, learned to figure, learned the
blade and learned the trigger
Learned what his other self already knew

The boy became the youth, the man, a man hid
from a youth who ran
From a boy's dark fright at a deep far light
A man shored up by shadow stuff
in double time at double bluff
Just fighting life and living for a fight

For that deep far light honed his sight as his
hearing tuned to the night
While anger rolled and rattled round his brain
By skin and the body bones caged
his nerve ends and arteries raged
Is pain the only thing to ease the pain

A voice sighed like a smoking gun, now listen good
there is no fun
This is as good as it will get by far
That voice cut like a Barlow knife, there is no other
better life
Believe me I'm your brother and your pa

The man became the thing he was because of this
and just because
And that's the way it happens, well I guess
It's kind of like that I should say, a bit like that
or that-away
Yeah, that's the way it happens more or less

When you're born out of a dying,

ghosts come round with truth and lying

And put you right and likewise put you wrong

That's the blood and that's the theory,

 thanks to all of you who hear me

That's the end of this interesting song.

CODA

PUB

Out on the wind's dumb roar
snow dust whirls like talcum.
Under Slieve League's dark jaw
there's talk and warmth and welcome.

We perch on stools in a tiny room
old bottles line the shelves.
Shadowed in the cozy gloom
we laugh amongst ourselves.

The pints, the whiskies come and go
the chat, the craic get better.
Down Bunglass road a slush stream flows
the night turns wet and wetter.

We are friends and travelers together
where sea and cloud go reeling.
Caught by weather or an angel's feather
beneath this smoky ceiling.

HEARTLAND

Looking East
that silly hillside pulls a face
two cottages for eyes
one turf-stack for a mouth.
South, the usual drunken sea.

I have learned much while here
rambling round your heartland dear.
Learned for instance, ease of talk
that the pine martin has a certain walk
that the moon's as lovely when a rind
that love's a lovely find
and all
while busy at your body
in my mind.

MEMORIAL STONE

a sonnet for Sinnet

i.m. David Sinnet Jones

A man dreams under a slate grey sky
Mad sea dreams that court derision
Plans and dreams with his one good eye
Half our sight, twice our vision

A man hauls bones, his slate bound bones
By hand, by will on a weed streamed yacht
Grapples with life where the green wind moans
In the deep salt spaces we would not

A man sails over a slate dark sea
Fumbles for breath, is humbled where
Horizons are a mystery
Denied to us who do not dare

Men are marked as lesser or as great
This man, nurtured by water, is honoured in slate.

BAPTISMS

1.
Today, a good start
a gathering, old stone
water even older
a certain sign.

Today these combine
to make you - maybe
Ryan Jack Nathaniel Rabey.

I smiled at that
and wish that you may also
- smile that is
and rhyme.

Yes, today - doubtless
a good start.

Away with you then
and welcome.

2.

Some love, some pain,

A life
that was the mother
becomes another.

And now
a dab of water

like no other

sets the dance.

The record turns.

Gently now
we place the stylus.

And
for Myla

the song begins.

ALMSBOX

I speak for a few of us as
entering perfection we find
it not quite that. The issued
silk provokes an unexpected
itch; this headgear weighs so
much. A persistent low unease
attends our steps, our progress
through the gilded air. We
move perplexed. Oh the funda-
mental right of it, the proper-
ness, we don't dispute. This is
the rest we've saved for, hope
we've earned, no doubt, no
doubt; just details bother us.
The light's a disappointment,
shot with dark; many of our
group seem, well.... rough. And
hardly the reward described
we feel - the educated dead
kept waiting at the gate
confronted with - copies of the
law, sad looks

and a locked box
blatantly marked
'Remember Ye Pore'

SONG WITH NO END

Is this the border sir to my new land?
I'm most glad to see you sir, where should I stand?
Could you repeat that sir? Ah, I understand.
Oh the small birds are all flown away.

Pardon me sir I'm somewhat lame
No sir I have no papers with my name
But here's a picture sir from where I came.
Oh the small birds are all flown away.

It's not that clear sir but you can just see
My son, my husband sir and there that's me
The papers sir? I'm sorry sir my memory.
Oh the small birds are all flown away.

Oh the small birds are all flown away
The sun, moon and stars don't belong
A feather drifts down through the day
On an earth that's unsung
From a sky without song
Oh the small birds are all flown away.

My papers sir? Excuse me sir I grieve
My husband had them I do believe
He would have kept them when we had to leave.
Oh the small birds are all flown away.

No sir, he was selected, one of ten
They stopped us, took away the strongest men
We heard some shooting sir and nothing then.
Oh the small birds are all flown away.

Yes sir my son also, that's very kind
No sir I'll wait just here sir I do not mind
I've time sir, all I have is left behind.
Oh the small birds are all flown away.

Oh the small birds are all flown away
The sun, moon and stars don't belong
A feather drifts down through the day
On an earth that's unsung
From a sky without song
Oh the small birds are all flown away.

THE PROCESSION

NOTE: These poems were written in response
to the series of figures "The Procession" created
by ceramic artist Meri Wells.

The italicised headings are largely drawn from the
artist's notes regarding that work.

The artist - catches sight of these creatures through the corner of the eye - almost always when they move in groups, endeavours to stabilise them - line first, then clay. The writer - scratches away.

in
front
is

bullcowhead
sweethorned

face nosesplit
hairblacked

minute
delicate
holes
to look out
to look in
eye to eye

bosom or
forehump

footloose

footless

robed in

mackintosh

greenhands

greengloved

hold spread

a day

or rule

or guide

or puzzle

book

or manual

check the place

in front

in place

to be continued

The glimpsed. No. Don't stare. Don't try. Why would you do that? The importance, value of the only ever to be glimpsed is enormous, beyond measure. No. Half see, half build, half write. They like that.

eyebluekissymouth

puck breasted

podge

damned tummy and
a rucksack lump
full of baby

ok wing-flips
(pigsealbird)
to swim/fly
proceed

she's
map-backed
a shawl
of birthmark
drapes
this way that

71

near twin near
her sister's
double packed
and bellybuttoned

siren
freckleheads
got floorfeet and
a backpedal

at ease with that
proceed

ro ro dumpies
on the ball

grace protected

grace fulfilled

They are all elders of their kind and have got to the position where they walk the world. Not for any reason but because that is what elders do. We might argue a reason. Might. If fool enough.

there have been

injuries

are deformities

some malevolence

hang dogs

bad

bunnies

perfectly

harmful

armless

this is not

a partner

ship

these

sail alone

aloof

one

skulled and

baleful one

with the

browser

mouth

one's got

the height look

one the deep

this is not

a partner

ship but

they'll help

each other

as

when

if

on

*There is little or no jockeying for hierarchy because they have all
got status. They are all equal in this and accept therefore each
other's validity. A bit like a collective. Bit.*

a beak

colour of

dura-glit

battery corrosion

functioning as

multi-purpose

tool or weapon

a ten point crown

obsolete

no function

a scrawled body

supporting

a hieroglyph hat

what's

a hieroglyph hat?

is the hat the body

are hearts and minds

within the headgear?

might it be

the hat information

is supplementary

to information/direction

kept/hid elsewhere

perhaps another

hieroglyph hat

where the glyphs

are illegible where

the hat has been

jammed *into* the

head not on

and

is all gold

old gold

evidence of fire

with

further evidence

of amputation

bodged punishment

hard and soft

damage

all smacks of
orders
transgression

is
bad regalia

They are elemental, each of its own particular place. Their traits could be cultural, geographical and yet - they borrow, swap, alter identity. Shape out of shape into shape.

some are snouted

some horned

one has a bashed up face

another is head-skinned

one has a wounded neck

none are ugly

many are burdened

with vessels and

wear collars, harness

helmets - devices to

assist their work

a club of hair

a massive stoop

act as strop

and hinge

a few have

forfeit limbs in

order to allow

the closer fitment

of this caparison
stoic feet grind
they get along

and the contents
never spill
the loads don't shift

what they haul

it is for ceremony
it is basic supplies

kindointment

foodwater

Some are magnetised (energised) by the group, others are not.
But they are all observers - observing the human condition as
they wend their way. The seeing - formalised.

fashionable and attractive

the weather girls

step outside

in oilskin berets

coats of penguin hide

nozzle noses raised

to test the air

to sniff the skies

coppered-gold antenna wave

siphon info. down

translate to travel news

of climate and terrain

it's like this

although inevitable

unstoppable

there are difficulties

to overcome

endure

and it is helpful

if some professions
certain defunct skills
are re-inhabited
so, weather girls
work jobs for life
they love it
clocked-in can click
on a sixpence
spit to forecast
divine and decide
buttonhole
what's what
they're at it now

under the sky's apron
uniformly
they brush the static
from their clothes

adjust the star collars
tuned
to tweak the universe

They are coming together in response to a pending crisis of our own making. These creatures have a common cause. They don't have to be elected, they just know. Go.

the equipment
is lugged
as body parts

great phono ears
(two measured lengths
of bright arterial cable
precision coiled
go into every set)

switchgear inserts
stitched to underskin

tracking aids
surgically attached

in.com implants
deep-graft meters/dials

these
fabulous technicians
are experts in the field
they sew and calibrate
as
the seams and circuits
pulse
are operational

mainframe scaffolding
of tensioned muscle
braces up the neck
the ribcage purrs
triangulates its
perforations

the head revolves
the chest vibrates

amped up
the speakers
blare their silence
perfectly

They have been travelling throughout the ages. They are mainly wise, some are elusive but they have all been chosen to journey towards a great gathering.

a gang

of young

of ghosts

so small

so pale

as though

for years

denied

all light

as though

just freed

from eggs

or dark

albino ancients

nurslings

wraiths

spirit brats

as old as

everything

absolved
of colour
they yet
define
colour

reject play
for pure
illumination

a chalk blush
deepening
in the glowing
skin

their dream
complexions

shine

They are aside from all things we see as human need and do not
require the same reassurances we do. They are not trying to save
the world and they do not suffer from human angst.

a few

go missing

get lost

in gardens

appear as

casualties

shambles and

dismemberment

but this should

not upset us for

they are not lost

as we are lost or

hurt as we are

hurt

they are not

poor stragglers

picked off

snares or snipers
have not
done for them
they've merely
side stepped
gone visible

are briefly
out of line
half-broke

reclined limbs
may drowse
in shrubbery
skins lounge
on the lawn
sleep-heads doze
on softwood stakes
mouth-traps yawn

no tragedy

potted torsos edge

the rockery

it's understood

they'll mend

be off

a half glance tells

they're only here

for good

What after the gathering? Maybe another gathering, maybe there never will be a gathering, maybe there can't be - why? For what reason - does it matter?

equality

is absolute

taken as read

neither shape

nor shade

here signify

precedence

innocence

or otherwise

nevertheless

there is one

black figure

wears an air

if not of high

superiority

then low key

decision making

would maybe

give the nod

were there a

question over
route or rest
or such

a skull-white
inseparable
companion
is just that
no more assistant
than another one
as all
proceed in throng
dash and potter on
glide and clamber on

the procession toils
to cart our baggage
minimise our damage

glimpse it when
you're eyebound
upon your special way

black figure merging white
blood-traits bound in clay
the procession wends
its path
your plight